W9-BAJ-739

Howler Monkey
Super Loud

by Natalie Lunis

Consultant: Dawn M. Kitchen, Ph.D.
Associate Professor, Department of Anthropology
The Ohio State University

BEARPORT
PUBLISHING

NEW YORK, NEW YORK

Credits

Cover, © Minden Pictures/SuperStock and © jaana piira/Shutterstock; TOC, © Blickwinkel/Huetter/Alamy; 4–5, © David Tipling/Nature Picture Library; 6T, © R. Wittek/Arco Images GmbH/Alamy; 6B, © Francois Gohier/Photo Researchers, Inc.; 7, © Minden Pictures/SuperStock; 9, © Lee Dalton/NHPA/Photoshot; 10, © Michael Fogden/DRK Photo; 11, © Minden Pictures/SuperStock; 12, © Thomas Marent/Ardea/Animals Animals Earth Scenes; 13, © Theo Allofs/Corbis; 14L, © Joel Sartore/National Geographic/Getty Images; 14R, © Joel Sartore Photography; 15, © Cortez Austin/NHPA/Photoshot; 16T, © Animals Animals/SuperStock; 16M, © Thomas Marent/Ardea; 16B, © Juan Carlos Muñoz/age fotostock/SuperStock; 17, © A. Mertiny/Wildlife/Peter Arnold/Photolibrary; 18, © Michael Turco; 19, © Piper Mackay/Nature Picture Library; 20, © Wolfgang Kaehler/SuperStock; 21, © Juniors Bildarchiv/age fotostock; 22, Royalty Free Composite; 23TL, © Joel Sartore/National Geographic/Getty Images; 23TM, © Minden Pictures/SuperStock; 23TR, © Dirk Ercken/Shutterstock; 23BL, © A. Mertiny/Wildlife/Peter Arnold/Photolibrary; 23BR, © Lee Dalton/NHPA/Photoshot.

Publisher: Kenn Goin
Editorial Director: Adam Siegel
Creative Director: Spencer Brinker
Cover Design: Dawn Beard Creative and Kim Jones
Photo Researcher: Picture Perfect Professionals, LLC

Library of Congress Cataloging-in-Publication Data

Lunis, Natalie.
  Howler monkey : super loud / by Natalie Lunis.
    p. cm. — (Animal loudmouths)
  Includes bibliographical references and index.
  ISBN-13: 978-1-61772-276-9 (library binding)
  ISBN-10: 1-61772-276-6 (library binding)
  1. Howler monkeys—Juvenile literature. I. Title.
  QL737.P915L86 2012
  599.8′55—dc22
                              2011002429

For more information, write to Bearport Publishing Company, Inc., 45 West 21st Street, Suite 3B, New York, New York 10010. Printed in the United States of America in North Mankato, Minnesota.

070111
042711CGB

10 9 8 7 6 5 4 3 2 1

Contents

A Loud Howl

High up in the treetops, as the sun comes up, a howler monkey is starting its day.

It opens its mouth, tilts its head back, and starts to howl.

The sound it makes is louder than the shrieks made by any other kind of monkey in the forest.

It is louder than the screeches, chirps, and whistles of all the birds in the trees.

In fact, it is one of the loudest sounds made by any animal in the world.

A howler monkey's howl doesn't sound like the howl of a dog or a wolf. It sounds more like a long, rumbling growl that turns into a roar.

5

Who's Howling?

Howler monkeys live in groups called troops.

Often, only one male monkey in the troop howls early in the morning.

Sometimes, however, two or more monkeys howl together.

The booming sound can be heard for at least a mile (1.6 km).

A howler monkey troop usually has between 4 and 15 members. One monkey, usually an older male, acts as the troop leader.

Stay Away!

A howler monkey's howl is hard to miss.

Other troops that are in the area hear it and answer with their own howls.

The loud sounds tell each group where the other monkeys are.

As a result, the howls actually help the animals protect themselves.

Hearing the sounds helps groups of howler monkeys avoid one another rather than fight over **territory**.

Howler Monkeys in the Wild

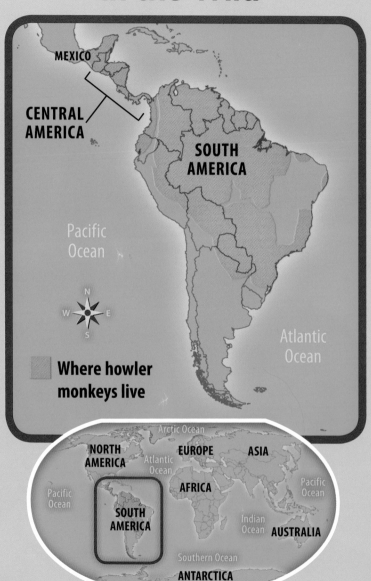

Where howler monkeys live

There are ten different species, or kinds, of howler monkeys. They live in **rain forests** in Mexico, Central America, and South America. The different species are known by the color of their fur—which may be black, brown, or red—and the place where they live.

Looking for Leaves

Once a troop of howlers knows that it has an area all to itself, the monkeys start to search for food.

They move through the treetops looking for leaves to eat.

If they are lucky, they will also find some tasty fruits, seeds, or flowers.

A howler monkey uses its tail to help hold on to branches as it travels through the trees.

tail

A Noisy Bunch

The monkeys in a troop stay mostly at the very top part of the rain forest when they travel from tree to tree.

That's where the freshest and tastiest leaves grow.

As they move around, they make many different sounds.

Adult males and females grunt and make clicking noises to check in with one another.

Baby howlers squeak and squeal as they play.

Good Grooming

Howler monkeys in a troop take care of one another.

One way they do this is through **grooming**.

They use their fingers to comb each other's fur.

Grooming helps keep the fur clean and smooth.

Although howler monkeys groom each other, they do not do so as much as other kinds of monkeys.

High-flying Enemies

Few kinds of animals are able to hunt howler monkeys high up in the trees.

Harpy eagles and other **raptors** are their main enemies.

When a member of a troop spots one of these fierce meat-eating birds, it lets out a loud scream.

The sound warns other howlers to watch out.

Other animals that might sometimes hunt and eat howler monkeys are jaguars, pumas, and boa constrictors.

jaguar

puma

boa constrictor

harpy eagle

Time to Sleep

Howler monkeys are not as fast and active as most other monkeys.

After gathering food in the morning, they spend the middle of the day resting.

Then they set out to look for more food.

A troop's day often ends with more howling that may let the other troops know where it is.

Finally, the howlers quiet down and go to sleep.

Howler monkeys spend almost all their lives in trees. One of the few times they climb down is to find water when they cannot get enough from the juicy leaves they eat in the trees.

baby howler monkey resting

19

Help for Howlers

Howler monkeys make lots of noise to protect themselves and their treetop territory.

However, there is one kind of danger they cannot stop.

Every year, many of the trees that they live in are cut down to make room for buildings, roads, and farmland.

Luckily, many people and groups are working together to save the animals' **habitat**.

By protecting the green, leafy rain forests, they will help make sure that the loudest voice in them will always be heard.

trees cut down for farming

Howler monkeys also face danger because some people hunt them for meat and capture them to sell as pets. People in many countries are working to make stronger laws to stop these actions.

Sound Check

Scientists measure how loud or soft sounds are in units called decibels. A howler monkey's howl measures around 90 decibels. That's about the same as the noise made by a gas-powered lawn mower. The chart below shows how this level of loudness compares to some other sounds.

Whisper
20 decibels

Normal Speaking Voice
60 decibels

Howler Monkey or Gas-Powered Lawn Mower
90 decibels

Train Engine
115 decibels

Rock Concert
120 decibels

Airplane Taking Off
140 decibels

Glossary

grooming (GROOM-ing)
cleaning

habitat (HAB-uh-*tat*)
the place in nature where an
animal or plant normally lives

rain forests (RAYN FOR-ists)
warm places where many trees
grow and lots of rain falls

raptors (RAP-torz) birds,
such as eagles and hawks, that
hunt and eat other animals

territory (TER-uh-*tor*-ee) an area of
land that belongs to and is defended
by an animal or a group of animals

23

Index

Read More

Donovan, Sandra. *Howler Monkeys.* Chicago: Raintree (2003).

Ganeri, Anita. *Howler Monkey.* Chicago: Heinemann Library (2011).

Reid, Mary E. *Howlers and Other New World Monkeys.* Chicago: World Book (2005).

Learn More Online

To learn more about howler monkeys, visit **www.bearportpublishing.com/AnimalLoudmouths**

About the Author

Natalie Lunis has written many science and nature books for children. She lives in the Hudson River Valley, just north of New York City.